YOU: A NOBLE ONE

Unleash the potential within

Dr. Dhirendra Kumar

Chennai • Bangalore

CLEVER FOX PUBLISHING
Chennai, India

Published by CLEVER FOX PUBLISHING 2025
Copyright © Dr. Dhirendra Kumar 2025

All Rights Reserved.
ISBN: 978-93-56480-84-1

This book has been published with all reasonable efforts taken to make the material error-free after the consent of the author. No part of this book shall be used, reproduced in any manner whatsoever without written permission from the author, except in the case of brief quotations embodied in critical articles and reviews.

The Author of this book is solely responsible and liable for its content including but not limited to the views, representations, descriptions, statements, information, opinions and references ["Content"]. The Content of this book shall not constitute or be construed or deemed to reflect the opinion or expression of the Publisher or Editor. Neither the Publisher nor Editor endorse or approve the Content of this book or guarantee the reliability, accuracy or completeness of the Content published herein and do not make any representations or warranties of any kind, express or implied, including but not limited to the implied warranties of merchantability, fitness for a particular purpose. The Publisher and Editor shall not be liable whatsoever for any errors, omissions, whether such errors or omissions result from negligence, accident, or any other cause or claims for loss or damages of any kind, including without limitation, indirect or consequential loss or damage arising out of use, inability to use, or about the reliability, accuracy or sufficiency of the information contained in this book.

Contents

Introduction .... *iv*

1. You: A Noble One 1

2. Power of Belief 7

3. Attitude is Ultimate 17

4. Succession Concept 27

5. Manage Your Habit 34

6. Upgrade Your Inner Self 41

7. Success Strategies 49

8. Now or Never 65

Introduction

You are a noble one. You are a beautiful creation of God. He has crafted you carefully. So, I am reminding you that you have immense potential to live a successful life. Success is simple, but you have made it complex. Follow the straightforward principles to succeed; you can undoubtedly win.

> *"Achievement is not your problem – alignment is."*
> **– Brendon Burchard**

Introspect deeply and sharpen your saw. Reorientation is the need of the hour. You have been performing under one mindset for too long. Your belief, courage, energy, emotions, and many more have been dis-aligned. You must have regularly been correcting your vehicle alignment in motor workshops. Sometimes your vehicle did not show any acute malfunctioning, even though you had gone to check whether your vehicle has proper alignment or not. Inside you, many activities are happening, which need to be corrected regularly; otherwise, you will be in trouble in your life's journey. Your vehicles are your asset. You know it very well, and if anything goes wrong with the vehicle, you check it and correct it. Yes, you know it very well, so you correct it regularly.

Are you aware that our valuable intangible assets are belief, courage, emotions, habits, determination, and many more? They are much more valuable than your vehicle, which leads your life's journey in a particular direction. They are essential for your improvement.

Are your present knowledge and awareness guiding you for proper improvement in your life?

You feel courageous, and perform better for some time, but soon go in vain. You may feel empowered for some time but after a few days again, you become dull and low. You may be trying an excellent activity for a long time, but it does not become a habit. How do you get consistency and sustained action for proper growth? Enjoy the power of the moment, as a seed (a tiny one) in its womb has infinite potential to become a full plant with leaves, flowers and fruits. A moment has infinite potential.

James Clear in his book *Atomic Habits*, highlighted the effect of shifting the route of an airplane by even a few degrees, and the destination of the plane gets shifted a lot. If one wants to go to a city named A but by shifting a few degrees, the plane gets landed in city B. In a similar way, a slight change in your daily habits can lead to a new horizon. Your one percent change in habit per day in the right direction get compounded into significant results. Success or failure is the product of your daily activities. So the money invested in a scheme gets compounded and gets multiplied in significant ways. Small changes in your daily activities result in compounded value. Habits categorize as ultra-high performer, high performer and low performer. No doubt everyone wants to be in the first category but it demands many sets of positive activities.

High performance requires some basic ingredients like goal setting, focusing on the target and measuring the route of achievement regularly. Why do we need the measurement?

To increase your productivity first, you should measure your goal; where you are now and where you want to go. Unless you measure your route, you will not be able to decide the path of the goal. Measure your energy, your strength and weaknesses, measure your capability and limits. Measurement provides clarity of your vision. You should make a scorecard of your strength and weaknesses, now decide whether you are looking for personal achievement, or for an organization or a project. If you are in the lead role of an organization and want the overall performance of the organization high, then you should do this for the team as well. You should work for the team. Make a mission statement of time in terms of weeks, months and years. Stick to it.

No doubt, you have a lot of aha moments, positive moments and days of success which are randomly distributed in your life. You never give attention to that. Now recollect, remind, rewrite on paper and then reanalyze. This act sparks your life. It provides how much successful you are. Of course, you have many successful moments. But due to unclear vision, your energy do not empower you to leap forward. I hope the takeaway is clear. It will reconnect and rewire your inherent potential. All ingredients and recipes are inside you. By reconnecting the wire of positivity, you may revamp your life. By this, no doubt, you will reinvent your new version.

High performers know their future and have a clear vision of the map to achieve it. They are sculpting themselves more regularly than others. No doubt, you have a lot of successes, aha moments, and victory points. These may be in different areas at different times of your life from your early childhood till date.

Here, I am uncovering the meaningful techniques of high performance. Experts have recommended to lessen the friction; lessen the friction in study, lessen the friction in relationships, lessen the friction in your financial planning, and lessen the friction in professional relations. If you follow this principle, it will result in more success. Do exercise with ease, do meditate with ease, and do your work with ease. Tap your physical energy, mental energy and spiritual energy and redirect in a particular direction.

I will try to highlight this in the coming chapters.

Of course, you can.

You will be a real achiever. You will live a joyful and triumphant life. The past has gone; don't pamper about the past. The present is pleasant.

Do you want to reorient/realign yourself holistically?

If Yes, be ready to reorient your life.

The journey starts now .

1
YOU: A NOBLE ONE

> *Come out into the Universe of Light. Everything in the Universe is yours; stretch out your arms and embrace it with love. If you ever felt you wanted to do that, you have felt God.*
>
> **– Swami Vivekanand**

You, yes, you! The beautiful creation of God. The same God who created the entire Universe. You are part and parcel of this Universe. The same energy flows inside you that flows in another successful person as well. You have come to the earth for a particular purpose. Believe in that. But you have put a curtain on your eye and crying for better. Shed or drop down the imaginary curtain. You and only you can make a change and make your life worthy. A slow or stagnant life is a sign of death. You are full of energy and enthusiasm. Go forward. Go forward.

The kingdom of God is within us. Of course, inside you, inside me, there is infinite strength. Stand up and hold on to the ground firmly. *Just focus the energy on* what *you want, and let the Universe do the rest.*

The Universe is under the influence of energy. The universal truth is "Energy is neither created nor destroyed." It only gets transformed. This is how everything is created, including you, your happiness, your positive emotions, your negative emotions, and many more. Everything is made up of energy, what you think, see, and even feel. You, including your beloved God and the entire Universe, are under the same wave of energy. Everything in your life, in my life, is created from energy. This energy is released in the form of your thoughts, words, and actions.

> *Change your thoughts, and you will change your world.*
> **– Norman Vincent Peale**

Thought – a pure and robust form of energy that changes you very quickly. It also makes ripples in the Universe, which ultimately creates and attracts the events and circumstances to your life. Thus, as you emit energy to the Universe you get power from the Universe. It is a two-way process. As you radiate the energy, you get the power. You and your happening are guided by these very principles. Again, as you emit as you receive. Like attracts like. Like thoughts attract like. One positive thought breeds into many. One dangerous thought also breeds into many more. You are using these very principles/laws of the Universe throughout your life. But you may not be aware of this.

> *There is enormous, generous energy in the Universe available to anyone who opens their hearts, minds, and souls.*
> **– Theresa Peluso**

So, open your heart and mind to receive the abundant energy to make your life happier and prosperous.

> *"Life does not consist mainly, or even primarily, of facts and happenings. It consists mainly of the stream of thoughts that is forever flowing through one's head."*
> **– Mark Twain**

> "...realize in your daily life that 'matter' is merely an aggregation of protons and electrons subjected entirely to the control of the mind; that your environment, your success, your happiness, are all of your own making... All wealth depends upon a clear understanding of the fact that the mind – thought – is the only creator. The great business of life is thinking. Control your thoughts, and you can control circumstances."
>
> **– Robert Collier**

Your body reflects/imparts what you eat, what you drink, and what you practice. You are mainly responsible for your body. You are the ruler of your body. If you don't take balanced and nutritious food, you won't be able to maintain your body. Be aware of your physical body and follow basic diet principles. Your body is also a building block of your personality, so don't let it loose. Be disciplined with your diet plan.

> *Follow your bliss, and the Universe will open doors where there were only walls.*
>
> **– Joseph Campbell**

You are the ruler of your mind.

You are the monarch of your soul.

You control and guide these three.

So, write your own rule and constitution.

Your life begins with you and ends with you.

The external journey is the manifestation of your inner road map.

> *"A man is what he thinks all day."*
> — **Ralph Waldo Emerson**

You are the game-changer of your health, your wealth, and of course, your excellence. You feel the timeless experience as you find the actual value of yourself. So, write your own rule and constitution to excel in your life.

> *You can have everything in life you want if you will just help other people get what they want.*
> — **Zig Ziglar**

> *"We are what our thoughts have made us, so take care about what you think. Words are secondary. Thoughts live; they travel far."*
> — **Swami Vivekanand**

You come alone in this world and will leave alone as well. Have extreme faith in yourself so you can make the work more pleasant.

Master your faith in yourself.

YOUR NOTES

2
POWER OF BELIEF

> *"We are what we believe we are."*
>
> **– C.S. Lewis**

What shapes our beliefs?

Unless you believe in your thought, you can't transform them into action. Unless you believe in your ability, you can't move ahead. Belief shapes the direction of your idea. Faith shapes your activity.

Belief is the button that triggers the action. One may be full of all the resources inside and outside, but belief begins the move.

It is the belief that blossomed inside Siddhartha (later he was known as Buddha) about 600 BC which led him to shed the royal legacy to work toward the human race. He guided humans in many ways to lead a peaceful life.

> *Faith is the bird that feels the light when the dawn is still dark.*
>
> **– Rabindranath Tagore**

Begin with belief

End with satisfaction.

Belief brings the brightness.

Believe in your physical strength. Believe in your mental soundness. Believe in your psychological wellness. So, believe in yourself. Let's think beyond the boundary. Most of the limitations are self-created. You, your environment, and your company knowingly or unknowingly created the boundaries. God is boundless. So, why do you think and act within the boundary?

Believe in your vision, so you may move with entusiasm.

> *"Be brave to stand for what you believe in even if you stand alone."*
>
> **– Roy T. Bennett,**

The world pattern is changing. No doubt, with the passage of time, it is becoming more prosperous. Visualize beyond what you can see.

How you turn unbelievable into believable?

Wilma Rudolph suffered from deadly diseases at a very early age, leading to paralysis. The doctor told her that she would never put her foot on the earth. Commitment with belief and hard work, she entered the race at 13, but she came last. She went into the second, third, and fourth races until she came first. Once she went to the coach named Ed Temple, she said, "I want to be the fastest woman on this earth."

Coach said, "With your spirit, nobody can stop you."

She beat others in 100 meters race and won her first gold medal. She beat others in 200 meters race and 400 meters race and won the gold medal. That suffered woman became the fastest woman on the earth in 1960. It is the belief. Yes, it is the belief which kept Wilma Rudolph going.

> *Seeds of faith are always within us; sometimes, it takes a crisis to nourish and encourage their growth.*
>
> **– Susan L. Taylor**

Believe in your ability every day. At the end of the day, belief wins. So, everyone keeps going from dawn to dusk to improve him or herself and his/her family as well.

How does this belief come?

As I interacted with several people from different walks of life in the last 16 years, which include working professionals, students of higher studies, and educated housewives, they reiterated working problems, strained relationships, friendship breakups, etc. They didn't talk about good friendships, a bright future, immense potential inside, tremendous working ability, beautiful nature, etc.

It's a great question. From where did this belief originate, and how did it develop?

It is a matter of research and careful observations of the masses. A vast group reeling under negativism.

> *In order to succeed, we must first believe that we can.*
>
> **– Nikos Kazantzakis**

Who/what should we blame?

Is it the environment?

Is it upbringing?

Is it friendship?

No doubt, negativism spread like wildfire.

If you are an older family member, carefully watch the environment inside the home, and who among the family members is more responsible for these. Form of negativism may be different. It varies from thought to action, from attitude to behavior. Our innocent children, teenagers, are very prone. Negative thinking should be pruned at the nascent stage as it proliferates.

Negative thoughts often stem from how others behave around us, which is a common aspect of human nature. So, we should be careful to prune it early. Otherwise, it becomes a monster. It is our moral duty to train our younger generations in this regard.

If such negative thoughts prevail for a longer duration, it becomes inherent, it turns into belief. If it becomes belief, it seems true. So, we should try to understand how the idea develops.

I can't manage the relationship breakup in friendship. I can't have a good friendship. These words are very common in society.

> *Faith is to believe what you do not see; the reward of this faith is to see what you believe.*
> **– Saint Augustine**

These are the few situations we constantly face in our society. But these are just a condition or concerns. You are not the only one who has come across such a situation. It is common. Analyze the life of a successful person. Who so ever you believe that he or she is successful, analyze the situation they faced. No doubt you will find that there were more harassing situations before them than your. So, face the situation boldly, before it becomes a belief that you cannot improve your condition. If you linger on the problem, it will lament your life badly.

Believe In Your Deed

Believe In Your Energy

Believe In Your Perseverance

Abraham Lincoln's story

1818: His mother died at the age of 9

1832: He lost his job

1832: Defeated in legislature election

1833: He entered business but failed

1834: He gets elected to the legislature

1835: His beloved one died

1836: Undergone nervous breakdown

1838: Defeated for Speaker election

1843: Lost for nomination for Congress

1848: Lost re-nomination

1849: Rejected for Land Officer

1854: Defeated for Senate

1856: Lost the nomination race for Vice-President

1858: Lost for Senate again

1860: Elected as President of the USA

What do you think?

Is it a story of success?

Or

Is it a story of failure?

He has been beaten up on different occasions, in a different field, at different times.

Why and how did he bounce back again and again? What were the ingredient and the inner values?

I think it was belief.

It was an example of sound belief, belief in his capability, belief in his power.

Elon Musk

You may call him an entrepreneur

You may call him one of the wealthiest people on earth

You may call him a great innovator

You may call him a risk-taker

Whatever you may call him, he is a living legend. A man of extraordinary intellectual courage. His vision is also beyond these planets. Intellectual courage is supported by hard work. SpaceX, *PayPal, Tesla.*

Long ago, in a dense forest, there was a competition among squirrels to reach the top of a hill. The goal was very tough as the way was very harsh. A big crowd was there to watch the race.

The race started; none believed that any of them would reach the top. The top was too high. They were shouting, "It is impossible to reach the top, so come back."

Most of them who came to watch the game thought it is very tough and that they shouldn't risk their lives. Even though some were moving, some looked back and came. Few slipped and died. Only one reached the top and won the race. Most of them wanted to hear the words of the winner. She didn't say anything; she was deaf. One of the reasons for winning the race was her inability to listen to the words the crowd was shouting.

> *Behind every success, there is belief.*
> *– Dhirendra Kumar*

Always think from the core of your heart and move ahead. Don't care about other advice or suggestions.

Visualization feeds your mind with meaningful messages. Your body will bloom. Ease your mind. Diffuse the tension.

Come out into an open space, which is usually calm. It may be a park or other such places. In the early morning, sit in the park with your legs crossed. Close your eyes.

Be calm and relax your body. Let your thoughts come and go. Whatever thoughts may be good or bad, don't resist. Take a few deep breaths. Be seated. Then visualize your surroundings, increasing the surrounding zone and expanding it slowly. Expand, expand and expand your visualization. Now visualize the atmosphere and the complete universe. Be calm and feel the whole Universe, including all planets, stars, galaxies, and many more. This is the origin of visualization.

Now realize, what is the significance of one person in this whole Universe? Is it smaller than a drop in the ocean? Even though God has chosen me and you to exist in this Universe.

You and I are significant to nature.

Am I very significant to nature?

Are you very significant to nature?

Yes, nature has chosen us to evolve.

> *"Create the highest, grandest vision possible for your life because you become what you believe."*
>
> **– Oprah Winfrey**

YOUR NOTES

3
ATTITUDE IS ULTIMATE

> *Your present circumstances don't determine where you can go; they merely determine where you start.*
>
> **– Nido Qubein**
>
> *Your attitude, not your aptitude, will determine your altitude.*
>
> **– Zig Ziglar**
>
> *Failure is an option here. If things are not failing, you are not innovating enough.*
>
> **– Elon Musk**

What Is Attitude?

Attitude is the way you think, the way you work, and the way you behave which ultimately impact how you perform. There are 24 hours for each person, but one is highly successful while the other is not. Attitude is one ingredient that changes the way one acts or works, or behaves. It is the fuel that guides you to *leap forward*.

Micro-changes in your action in a positive direction improve your progress. Whatever you do when you arise in the morning until you sleep determines your progress. Success is not a one-day process.

> *But what you do in one day determines your progress.*
>
> **– Dr. Dhirendra Kumar**

Success is a continuous process. One should not look upon it in isolation. Your daily activities mark an impression on the path to success. The daily activities determine the direction of your progress.

Here, I request you to stop reading this for 5 to 10 minutes. Sit in a comfortable position. Sit with ease. Close your eyes. Review/relook at the way you do your professional work.

> *That has been one of my mantras for focus and simplicity. Simple can be more complicated than complex. You have to work hard to get your thinking clean to make it simple.*
>
> **– Steve Jobs**

Steve Jobs – a tech-savvy man who changed the game of innovation in technology. He totally revolutionized Apple. He took care of everything, minute detail from manufacturing, packaging, advertising, and consumer satisfaction. His working style reflects his attitude. He demands and command elegant simplicity and perfection. He favored performance with perfection. He never compromised on quality and price. He invented the cutting-edge technology of the time.

As was his product, as was his attitude – advanced and transparent. Several case studies and research on his working ability and style revealed that his primary focus was on futuristic technology with simplicity. **His product is not only a brand, but his attitude is also a brand.**

> *Your time is limited, so don't waste it living someone else's life. My job is to not be accessible to people. My job is to make them better. Your work will fill a large part of your*

> *life. The only way to be truly satisfied is to do what you believe is great work. And the only way to do great work is to love what you do. If you haven't found it yet, keep looking. Don't settle. As with all matters of heart, you will know when you find it.*
>
> – **Steve Jobs**

Attitude reflects your mindset.

It is a predisposition or a tendency of an individual to respond to a specific idea, object, or situation. They may respond either positively or negatively. Attitude guides a person's choice of motion.

Attitudes are dictated by various factors. We can also have different attitudes towards the same thing or the same situation and produce different attitudes.

Most people are not aware of their attitudes.

An attitude is the response of a person to people, environment, society, events, and circumstances in different situations.

No matter, in what situation you are now, in which condition you are now, whether you are prosperous or poor, whether you are healthy or ill.

You can change your attitude and be a winner.

Yes, change your attitude, which changes your perception, which changes your response and degree of response as well.

If you think negatively, turn it to positive,

If you are positive, be more … more positive.

Positive and only positive, so you can turn the tide in your favor on your side.

> *"The person who goes farthest is generally the one who is willing to do and dare. The sure-thing boat never gets far from shore."*
> **– Dale Carnegie**

> *Expect the best. Prepare for the worst. Capitalize on what comes.*
> **– Zig Ziglar**

Once a bird asked a honey bee, "After continuous hard work you prepare the honey. But a man steals the honey. Do you not feel sad?"

Then the bee replied, "Never … Because a man can only steal my honey, not my art of making honey."

> *Ability is what you are capable of doing. Motivation determines what you do. Attitude determines how well you do it.*
> **– Lou Holtz**

Have a positive attitude, whatever happened in past, don't bother, but take massive action now.

If you want to change the attitude comprehensively, you have to be aware of your thought process, your environment and your friendship.

No doubt, every person comes across success and defeat, ups and down; adversity and pleasant moment.

But, the important thing is how a person responds to it, which is mainly determined by attitude. You cannot change how people react to you but how you respond to people is at your hand. Nelson Mandela, when imprisoned for years, was neither depressed nor down. He responded positively and remained attached to the principle of freedom struggle. Gandhi Ji was once thrown out from a train in South Africa.

If you were there instead of Gandhi Ji, what would be your reaction in that situation?

Just think for a moment.

> *You cannot control what happens to you, but you can control your attitude toward what happens to you, and in that, you will be mastering change rather than allowing it to master you.*
>
> **– Brian Tracy**

In such a situation, a common man would have been angered or depressed. But, he took it as a challenge, and with rational planning, he struggled to provide freedom to India.

That is the difference between a normal person and a person with zeal.

That is the difference in perception.

That is the difference in mindset.

That is the difference in looking at a situation.

How do such differences occur among people? It is mainly due to cultural background, education, commitment, determination, etc.

Every day apple drops from the tree to the ground, but it was perceived differently by Newton.

> *People may hear your words, but they feel your attitude.*
> **– John C. Maxwell**

What is an attitude? An attitude may be the way how you react to a situation. An attitude has three components. An attitude is made up of:

- What you think/imagine.
- What you do/react to.
- What you feel/perceive.

Everyone reacts to a particular situation in a different way. Everyone has different perceptions about a particular situation. But broadly, it may be classified as negative or positive.

The thing that obstructs, also opens up many opportunities. As adversity advances, it is up to you how you perceive and react. It provides you a platform to bounce back, no doubt, bounce back for the betterment. Thought, belief, and words determine the action you take. Thought is a form of energy which has incredible power, which can change the words you speak, and it can change the belief you have. It's an ordinary saying, "Life begins at the end of the comfort zone." Most people think that a comfort zone means a zone of physical activities and physical movement.

But here, I would like to emphasize the importance of stepping out of the comfort zone of your thoughts, beliefs, and speech.

Most of the population is inside the thought process of the comfort zone. They don't dare to think beyond their comfort zone. Physical activities or actions come later. Try to stretch your thought process properly.

> *Excellence is not a skill; it's an attitude.*
> **– Ralph Marston**

The seed of opportunities grows as adversity advances. It is up to you how you look over the situation. Whether you engage yourself in trouble or water the seed of opportunities hidden inside the adversity. Many times, in life, such situations arise. Adversity allows us to review the conditions, which guides us on what went wrong. It opens up the treasure of hidden potential.

Doing the work beforehand proactively, is the winner attitude; persons with winner attitudes do beautiful things. It is a time-tested experiment. Just by changing his attitude, a man can do wonderful things. The loser attitude leads to a life full of sorrow; they see only the hurdles in every task.

Attitude reflects your mindset. A predisposition or a tendency of an individual to respond towards a certain idea, object, person, or situation. They may respond either positively or negatively. Attitude guides a person's choice of action. Attitudes are dictated by various factors. We can also have different attitudes towards the same thing or the same situation produces different attitudes among people.

So, one should cultivate a positive attitude to become successful in life.

YOUR NOTES

4
SUCCESSION CONCEPT

> *There is surely nothing other than the single purpose of the present moment. A man's whole life is a succession of moment after moment. If one fully understands the present moment, there will be nothing else to do, and nothing else to pursue. Live being true to the single purpose of the moment.*
>
> **– Yamamoto Tsunetomo**

Success is not just repeating the same act for work, time and again.

The succession concept includes an act, idea and thoughts which trigger another set of actions, idea, and thoughts, which further forms a chain of reaction. The reaction may be in the form of action, thought or behavior, etc.

You must have experienced this even when you take action positively. You feel empowered and more similar thoughts come to your mind. Whenever one gets involved in a negative act, a series of similar thoughts also hits your mind. So, be careful about this and practice it in your life.

> *Life is a succession of moments, to live each one is to succeed.*
>
> **– Corita Kent**

Failure Succession Cycle

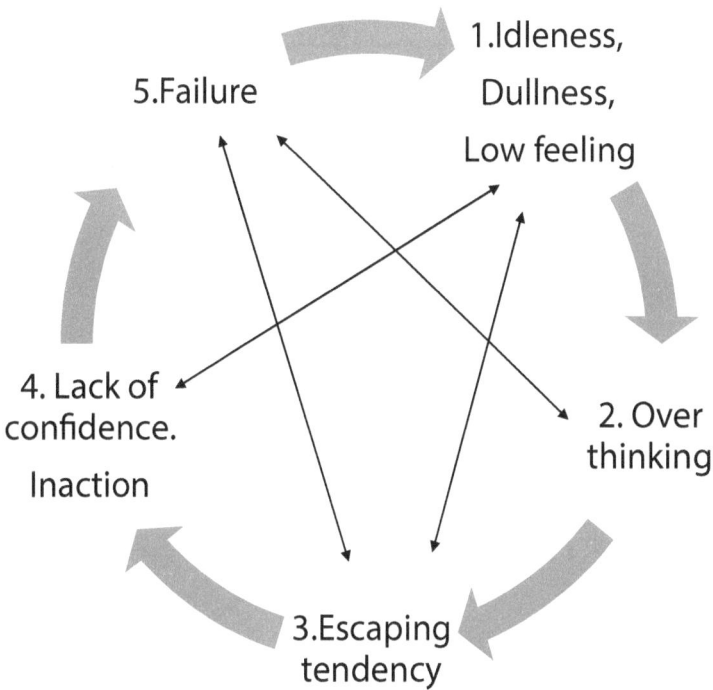

Failure Succession Cycle- Idleness and dullness lead to low feeling and over thinking which further breeds escaping tendency, lack of confidence and inaction which finally culminate into failure. It's an inter-woven and interlinked cycle. This condition prevails slowly and silently. If you keep watching yourself then only you may understand this. Passive habits are more prevalent.

Action Habit	**Passive Habit**
Start himself/herself.	Wait to get started by others.
Idea followed by execution.	Idea followed by no action.
Believe in working now.	Postpone for tomorrow.

One idea followed till the result.	One idea followed by another idea but no execution.
Do it now habit.	Put for tomorrow then tomorrow.
Always enthusiastic.	Idleness.

Virtuous Cycle of Success

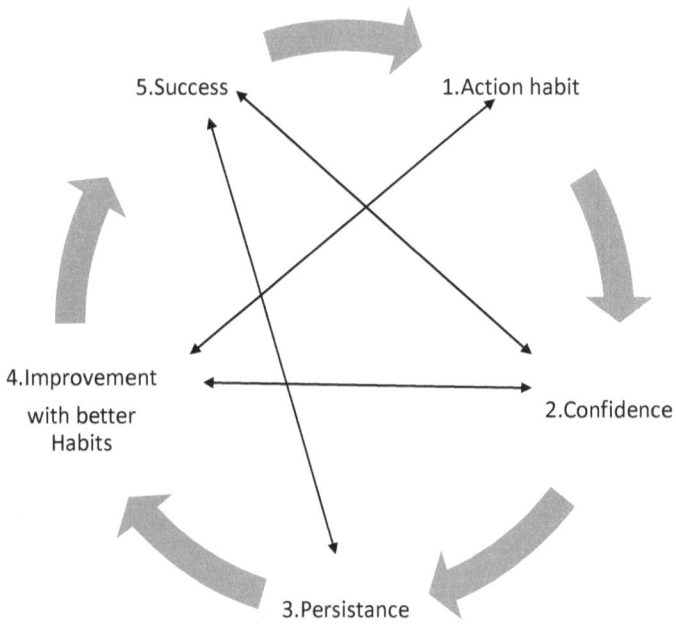

If you take action or massive action, which leads to confidence, persistence, better habits and finally success. These are sequential and inter-linked. Be consistent in your work, irrespective of all odds, so it breeds positivity and consistency.

> *Nature gives to every time and season some beauties of its own; and from morning to night, as from the cradle to the grave, it is but a succession of changes so gentle and easy that we can scarcely mark their progress.*
>
> **– Charles Dickens**

The Virtuous Cycle of Success remains away from those who don't like sweat and blood. Don't limit your imagination. Imagine wildly and imagine beyond your limit. Go above the intelligence levels. Work hard as work is worship. Since you have this book in your hand, this shows you must have a burning desire, a great vision, a mission, a dream and a goal.

These are in the form of energy as they may fade away with time. Keep them in proper form to achieve it, which requires, one thought, one mission, and one vision at one time till the final.

Finish the work in time or time will finish you.

No doubt, you have a great dream. It is better to plunge into action than to wait for a favorable time to come. No doubt you have done a lot of mental practice, dream, planning, etc. All these practices are good but results come out when you execute them.

> *There is no royal road to anything, one thing at a time, all things in succession. That which grows fast, withers as rapidly. That which grows slowly, endures.*
>
> **– Josiah Gilbert Holland**

Change the Cycle

How to Change a Vicious Cycle of Failure into a Virtuous Cycle of Success

Believe in the following principle.

Action leads to spirit.

Inaction leads to frustration.

As much as you work, you will be able to work extra. Darwin's evolution theory also suggests as you work more, you get more strength. A zone of action confers the space or zone where you work efficiently without much effort. It includes professional duty, family engagement, sport, and hobby hunting.

YOUR NOTES

5
MANAGE YOUR HABIT

> *Habit heals if it is good. Habit haunts if it is bad.*
> *Habit makes you a winner if it is good.*
> *Habit makes you a sinner, if it is bad.*
>
> **– Dr. Dhirendra Kumar**

Anything repeated regularly, becomes a habit. If you practice good things regularly, then it becomes a good habit. If one practices bad things regularly, then it becomes a bad habit. So, whatever is repeated regularly for a particular period of time, becomes a habit. So, to get it into our subconscious mind, it should be repeated regularly. A practice which is done regularly becomes a habit. Action which we perform regularly for some time gets engraved in our personality. It gets engraved in such a way that our physiology gets trained in this fashion. So, repetition of any work or regular practice of a particular action leads to habit.

Our body or physiology does not understand which is good or bad, whichever action is repeated regularly becomes a habit. So, it is up to us to keep attention on every action we perform regularly. It is scientifically proven by the Pavlov experiment.

> *A habit cannot be tossed out the window; it must be coaxed down the stairs a step at a time.*
>
> **– Mark Twain**
>
> *Discipline is choosing between what you want now and what you want most.*
>
> **– Abraham Lincoln**

What you do with ease at regular interval of time becomes habit. If an act is repeated time and again there may be a chance, it becomes a habit. Tiny action produces the compound effect in due course of time along with major results. Small behavioral changes mark a new dimension in habit forming. You may have experienced that you are doing some work with ease without much thought.

Such acts get repeated and in due course of time, it becomes a habit.

It gets inscribed in our biological system. People enjoy doing such activities. It works under the effect of dopamine which forms a repetitive cycle. Be careful/watchful over your own activity, you may understand how a particular habit becomes part of your life. The act by which you are rewarded or by doing an act you feel pleasure, you repeat it again and again which generally becomes a habit. Habit is of different kinds but broadly it may be classified as a good habit or bad habit. Good habits are those which improve your health, finance, education, and relationship. The activities which improve your health include exercise, walking, yoga, meditation, proper medication, etc.

Financial discipline with a proper habit of investing is of prime importance in the present time as a lot of investing ads lure you. The habit which strengthens your financial position includes proper planning of investing and regular saving. Saving is the key to financial discipline. It works in a similar way: caring nature and mutual respect strengthen the relationship. The effect of each habit gets compounded, no matter whether the habit is good or bad.

> *Feeling sorry for yourself, and your present condition is not only a waste of energy but the worst habit you could possibly have.*
>
> **– Dale Carnegie**

In one line it may be said life is a total of your habits. Habits may be good or bad, worse or worthful. Make good habits possible and bad habits impossible with tiny changes.

Habit Score Card

The direction of your life is steered by the habit you have. So, making the score card of habits measure your life trajectory. Make a table of your good habits and bad habits. Provide a score for each based on your knowledge, and analyze where there is scope for improvement. Don't overthink it; keep going. Keep things that you want to refrain from out of your reach. Our life is short on this planet, so time management is essential for both personal and professional growth.

Measure where you are now and where you want to go. And what is your target. If you let your life easy going without any perfect goal, there will be chances that you may get trapped in bad habits. Bad habits are addictive in nature because it provides quick pleasure. If you choose a bad habit or get trapped in a bad habit your life becomes messy and hard. In contrast, if you follow good habits, your life would be in the right direction. Now questions arise how to choose or change the habit. If you try to pick a new habit which is beneficial for your life, first make it easy and accessible. Start by dedicating a very small amount of time to it so that interest develops naturally over time. Make the environment conducive for it, and gradually increase the time spent on the activity. Make it attractive and easy to work with.

The cycle of habit formation is a complex interplay of various factors that influence our behaviors. The environment, for instance, plays a crucial role as it can trigger or discourage certain habits. A tidy and organized space may promote productivity, while a cluttered one might lead to procrastination. Friends and family also significantly impact habit formation; their behaviors can serve as models for our own. If a family values healthy eating, an individual is more likely to adopt similar habits. Society at large sets norms and expectations that can shape habits; for example, cultural norms around meal times or exercise can lead to the establishment of related routines. Understanding these factors can help in creating strategies to form new habits or alter existing ones. It's a delicate balance where each element can either support or hinder the development of a habit loop, which consists of a cue, a routine, and a reward.

These factors influence your habit either directly or indirectly. If you want to be a sportsman then follow the habit of a sportsman. If you want to be an academician follow the habit of an academician. Don't waste much time on trial and error. It is better to follow the principles of successful people. Many people have asked me during my career counseling journey, how to be away from bad habits. Escaping from bad habits involves a strategic approach where making the habit unattractive plays a crucial role. This can be achieved by associating negative consequences with the habit, thereby reducing its appeal. Additionally, distancing oneself from environments or social circles that encourage the bad habit is equally important. By creating a supportive environment that fosters good habits, and by consistently reminding oneself of the benefits of staying away from harmful practices, one can gradually replace negative behaviors with positive ones. This process requires patience, persistence, and often, the support of friends, family, or professionals.

Successful people are simply those with successful habits. -**Brian Tracy**

YOUR NOTES

6
UPGRADE YOUR INNER SELF

Upgrade Your Inner Self

Life is lovable if you know the basic principle of living and personal improvement techniques and practice it regularly. Life will be miserable if you do not follow the basic principles.

Life involves a myriad of opportunities and challenges. It's a life journey where every individual encounters their own set of circumstances, some favorable and some not. The beauty of life lies in the diversity of these experiences. Opportunities often come disguised as obstacles, and it's our approach or our attitude towards them that determines our path. Embracing life's beauty involves recognizing the potential in every moment, good or bad, and understanding that each experience is a step towards growth. It's about finding joy and meaning in both the opportunities and oppositions that life presents. Ultimately, the quality of our lives is greatly determined by our perspective, attitude and the choices we make in response to what life offers us.

Upgrading your belief-system and your mindset, are very important for success in every walks of life.

The belief system and mind set do not develop in a day or two but it takes a long duration of time. We don't realize how it develop but it is taking shapes inside us. It is working as a software which works inside the digital device.

Paradigm Matters

It is perception or may call it is an assumption that you have for a particular thing, situation, or condition. It may be your way of thinking, your way of working your way of analyzing the situation. Different people may have different perception to same situation or condition. Your paradigm reflects how you proceed towards your goal or destiny. How is it different from persons to persons? It is mainly determined by the education, experience, parenting and many more like social moral and ethical values that one possess. If you understand your paradigm then analyses it properly, so you can improve in a better way. One may compare it with map or tour guide, if it is right, you will reach the destiny in proper way with least effort. Your view is very important for your improvement. So have time to look after your view of life. Your paradigm guides your attitude, behavior and working potential.

Action Habit

If you want to succeed in your life act immediately towards your goal. Success needs action. Action in a focused way. Focused actions require straight thinking. Focused and consistent efforts mark the progress in right way. Habit of action is the focus point of successful persons who improve their life.

Beat the Procrastination

The dark side of our personality is procrastination. It is inherent in your persona, which silently takes its shape.

It is the common habit that we put the things for tomorrow, then for day after tomorrow and even after that. We don't become active unless it is very urgent. It's in our habit that we make simpler thing very harder by putting it for next time. Make a plan or system to work. This system should be your own not of the organization you are working in. Here, I am talking about personal working system which is different from professional work culture or system. Here, I am emphasizing on personal work culture or system that is to be developed by you own self. It is very important for personal improvement. Hold the life by its horn. Don't let it loose.

It's a common perception, time is infinite, so will do the work at hand next time. But in reality life is short and time is very limited. Even though we don't care for days, weeks and even months. if one day slips from your life, you missed a lot.

Passion is the enemy of Procrastination. If you are passionate or interested in doing something, you don't miss the opportunity. Great works can be achieved only through passion and perfection. Where there is passion, positivity prevails.

Make the things attractive and interesting which ever things that you want to do.

Getting things done is new mantra. Build your own system outside and inside to work.

If your boss gives you any task that is needed for profession and you don't like it, then don't think much or don't think extra but act on it. Immediate action is needed, Action clears your mind and remove the unwanted thoughts. As you think more, you become more scared about it. When you start acting on it then you feel good after some time. It is in the nature itself.

Synergy of desire, dream, and determination

> *Dream as if you'll live forever. Live as if you'll die today.*
> **– James Dean**

The desire, dream and the determination are the few major component of your inner self, if these work in proper way, it does miracle in your work. Synergistic effect of desire, dream, and determination lead for the immediate actions. If you want to design your destiny, then follow the principles of regular and consistent work.

Don't say sweet dream. A dream of night becomes futile in the day.

So, work hard to make dreams come true. The dreams that come on the pleasant night, vanishes as sun rays fall on it. Day dreamer, who think beyond the boundary and work out of their comfort zone, make the globe glow. It is human nature to be in the zone of comfort, so analyze your situation and take immediate action accordingly.

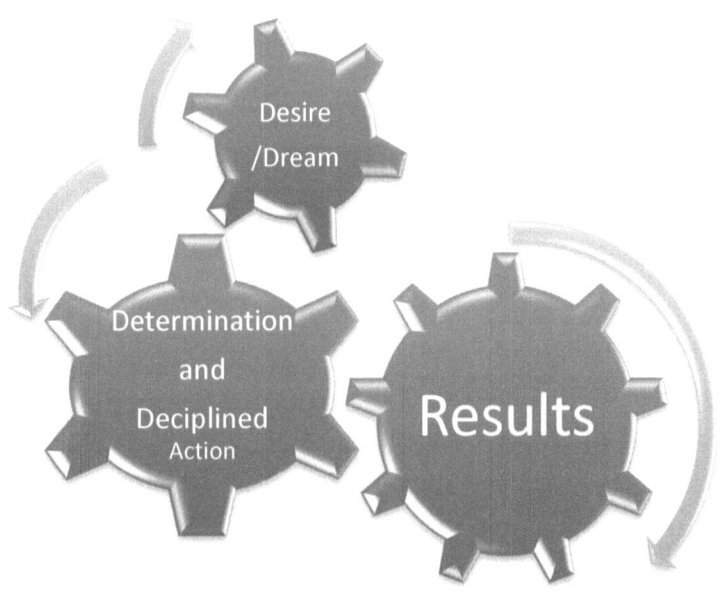

A man was born into a poor family. His unique vision redefined the potential of the Indian corporate sector. He was confident that finance would never be a constraint in executing his projects. **A man** dares to dream and learn to excel. He revolutionized the capital markets of India. This man was Dhirubhai Ambani. In his words, "Our dreams have to be more significant. Our ambitions are higher. Our commitment is deeper. And our efforts are more remarkable. You do not require an invitation to make profits.", "Meeting the deadlines is not good enough; beating the deadlines is my expectation", and "Don't give up; courage is my conviction."

A true story of a dream, desire, and determination.

There was an uncommon man dreamt of doing for the common men and the common cause. His dream and determination define the destiny of the very commoner. He defines the new way of politics. He provided a new paradigm in democracy. This was M.K Gandhi, father of the nation of India.

TAKE OUT some TIME FOR YOURSELF

If for the whole day, you are involved in your work and you do not manage time for yourself to think for yourself, a few quiet moments are very essential for your desire and dream to flourish. Sometime during the day, sit calmly for a few minutes, with your eyes closed, look inside, and keep away your worldly thoughts. Try to be flexible. Refusal refills your energy. Shed your mental garbage daily. As you are calmer, more positive thoughts and desires come to you. Creativity springs up when you are calm and relaxed. You need to renounce the physical world for some time to enhance creativity.

The world needs dreamers, and the world needs doers. But above all, the world needs dreamers who do.

– Sarah Ban Breathnach

YOUR NOTES

7
SUCCESS STRATEGIES

> *Don't judge each day by the harvest you reap but by the seeds that you plant.*
> — **Robert Louis Stevenson**

What is success?

What does it mean to you? It differs from person to person, place to place, and from one society to another. Even a particular individual redefines and re-evaluates the definition of success with the passage of time.

The purpose of life is to improve. No one should deviate from this very principle. Desire, commitment, hard work and positivity improve efficiency with winning instincts.

For activeness you need:

- Physical workout
- Emotional workout
- Spiritual workout

Whatever you like to be, don't doubt you would be

If you want to be a CEO, you should think and grow like one. If you want to be an entrepreneur, you should think and grow as an entrepreneur.

Enrich your thought

Enrich your action

Enrich your attitude

And enrich your vision.

Redesign your thought now,

Improve your vision today,

Rediscover yourself now.

Diminish the demon inside you.

Explore the energy inside you.

Inside you, a lot of energy resides.

> *All power is within you. You can do anything and everything. Believe in that. Do not believe that you are weak; do not believe that you are half-crazy lunatics, as most do nowadays. Stand up and express the divinity within you.*
>
> **– Vivekananda**

Tailor your fortune in your personal lab. How dream or desire arises? Those who have a desire or dream can move ahead. No doubt, wild imaginations make life civilized. History hails only those human being who dares to go beyond their limits. Shed your fixed mental boundaries. Break down the physical limitations. Open up your spirit. Only those who dare to diminish the fixed rule of their time either in science, art, medicine or space made the world happier.

A small boy, born into a normal family, wandered many places with or without any purposeful vision. Sometimes he stood at a roadside stall for his livelihood while many times moved to other places. At that time, no one cared about his fate. With his desire to move and go ahead, shedding the criticism, shedding the negative comments, he moved faster to go ahead. With time, he changed his makeover, which fit in. Many times, he bounced back and went ahead till he reached a new height. This may be the journey of every winning people, who you think is successful in your view.

Steve Jobs, Abraham Lincoln, Barak Obama, Nelson Mandela, M.K. Gandhi and many more reflect similar stories.

Golden Rules of Success

- Never give up
- Never lose heart
- Like what you do
- Don't listen to a little-hearted man
- Listen to inner voices
- Do something important
- Look for a solution of a problem
- Associate with great people
- Work super harder

How Desires/Dreams Arise

If you try to understand how desire/dream arises in an individual, you will be able to design your destiny. Many factors are very important or significant to determine the shape of the dream which include environment, culture, family, wisdom, and individual aspirations.

If a desire or a dream comes into your mind, you feel energized and you would be ready to do work fast.

God has faith in you. So, he has given the different ideas, enormous dreams, and desires to you. You must nurture the desire and dream to make them into shape. Don't let it to be vanished.

Why you? Why He has so much faith in you for such works?

No doubt, you will work with greater energy, focused concentration and with much determination. No doubt, reviewing your work is good but don't overthink. Success seekers never look back. Whatever has been done is done. No regret. No pain. Do not relook what has been done. Go ahead! If you repent or regret. You lose energy. You lose commitment. You lose your faith in yourself.

Swap the year into the month

Swap month into week

Swap week into today

Swap today into *now*

Now has great significance in our life to accomplish an excellent work. There has been a great significance of the present moment from time immemorial. Making a list of works is a good idea. Most people plan for a year, for a month or for a week but not for today. This is the problem, so, I suggest you make a plan for today and then see the true results. If you have a plan for a longer time span, it remains on your list year after year. So, try to shrink the list to finish the work today or even now; otherwise, it remains so far, and you would not be able to finish.

Enjoy the work

Work to enjoy.

When you are upset or dull or don't like to work.

At that moment,

Change the posture

Change the position

Close up your eye and stand up.

Have a deep breath *inside and out.*

Now you do the job you have.

Go ahead with the job you have.

Time Management

Benjamin Franklin observed, "There will be plenty of time to sleep when you are dead." It is an accurate account of life. It is an excellent message to improve life.

Life is full of opportunities and a lot of work to be done. As more you waste your time, the more you become lazier. People mainly waste their time sleeping and gossiping. It is up to you to manage the time. Sleep is essential for health, rejuvenation, and making a fresh start. A lot of sleep makes you lazy and bored. The demarcation line needs to be defined. How much do you need sleep? It depends on several factors like the food you eat, physical exercise, yoga, and meditation that you practice. Junk food makes you sleepy. Not the quantity, but the quality of sleep is of utmost importance. The duration of sleep varies from person to person. Many people manage to have only four hours of sleep. Vivekanand manages his life only on four hours of sleep. Gandhiji followed a strictly disciplined life, so he had complete control over his sleep. He can switch the sleep pattern as he likes to follow. This type of sleep pattern requires a lot of practice. How to manage this needs guidelines and rules to follow.

Daily routine

It generally involves every detail that is to be followed for a day. First, draw a broad outline of the day that is to follow. Go for detail and whatever detail that one design must follow it for at least 21 days so that it may become inherent. Make your own daily routine considering every minute's detail. Allow every thought to come and put them on paper.

Life is to enjoy

Life is to work

Life is to explore

Life is to be great

Life is to improve.

Time and tide wait for none. Time slips very fast from your hand. Better to do it now for those who want to excel significantly in life.

Steve Jobs once pondered about one of the most considerable time management techniques. You may say it may change your thought process. He pointed out, "What would I do if this was the last night of my life?" It has great potential to invoke a new trend in behavior patterns. Don't be trapped by dogma- which is living with the results of other people's thinking. Don't let the noise of other's opinions drown out your own inner voice. And most important, dare to follow your heart and intuition.

> *For the past 33 years, I have looked in the mirror every morning and asked myself: 'If today were the last day of my life, would I want to do what I am about to do today?' And whenever the answer has been 'No' for too many days in a row, I know I need to change something.*
>
> *– Steve Jobs*

Persons who wait for the actual time to start their work, wait forever. Proper time never comes. Do not wait for the perfect time to launch a project. It never comes. It is just an excuse. Better to do it now for those who want to excel significantly in life. Don't overthink the start and execution. Excess thought is not required for a start. Better to do it now for those who want to excel in life. Don't overthink the start and execution. If you wait for the perfect environment to begin, you'll end up waiting indefinitely. You might have observed that in this society, a lot of people wait to start a new project. There is always a theme in life: don't wait and don't be late.

Don't put the thing in your mind or brain for a longer duration; things may become messier or wipe out, so write it on paper. Do plan and organize the thing on the paper. Writing on paper is a wonderful practice to ease the work. Writing means crafting, so writing removes uncertainty.

A better technique to do the thing in better way.

To manage time, follow 3 P

Provocative

Prioritize

No Procrastination

Body

The body promotes your performance if it is sound and healthy; it helps you in your career journey, professional journey, and spiritual journey. A lousy body hurdles progress. Think of your body as healthy; you feel a sense of excitement and you do work efficiently. But think when there was any pain in any part of your body, your attention goes always to that very part, and you could not focus on work. If the pain is acute, you won't be able to perform at all. If anyone becomes ill chronically, it costs a lot in terms of money and time. It leads to countless losses. But at the present time, don't give attention to these things. Just think about it and start trying to make it healthy and sound. Health is a manifestation of what and how you eat, drink, and breathe.

> *Start by doing what's necessary; then do what's possible; and suddenly, you are doing the impossible.*
>
> **– Francis of Assisi**

Food is fuel

What kind of food you eat determines what kind of body you get. There are different kinds of food preferred or meant for people in different professions. Some professions require much more physical activity while, others require significantly less. What kind of food our body requires depends on our activities. When we eat a particular food, we feel energetic, comfortable and enthusiastic. In another way, when we eat some popular type of food, we feel lethargic, dull and depressed. What amount of food you eat, the quality of food you eat, and at what time you eat determine body performance and growth. Emotions are tied to our body's performance and growth. If you eat healthy food but you are under acute and negative thoughts/emotions like fear, anger, etc., you must have realized how it negatively acts inside your body. Liquid or what you drink also has a massive role in the performance of our body.

> *Being deeply loved by someone gives you strength, while loving someone deeply gives you courage.*
>
> – Lao Tzu

Breathing

It is essential for life. If it stops, life ceases. You must understand how important it is. Every time we need it, so its importance is much more than food and water. We give attention to what we eat and what we drink, but ordinary people ignore the significance of breathing. It is the breathing by which we get oxygen inside and release toxic gases from our bodies. This is needed by every cell of our body. Oxygen is essential for metabolism and different physiological function of different cells of organs. With the help of yoga practices, physical exercises, and meditation (by following proper breathing techniques), one can improve overall health under expert guidance.

> *You cannot swim for new horizons until you have the courage to lose sight of the shore.*

Understand the value of the subconscious mind

Have you ever tried to understand why someone is so efficient in work and gets successful? Someone is so healthy and joyous, while others are sad and less productive. Why one has beautiful and successful life while the other is dull and depressed? Joseph Murphy, in his book, *Power of Your Subconscious Mind*, highlighted that one may improve health, wealth and relationship. But the question arises on how to improve our health, wealth and relationship, behavior and, of course, attitude. First, understand and realize what the subconscious mind is. It is eternal universal and permanent. It prevails in all individuals. It always guides for perfection and improvement. It is powerful and mends your life in the right direction. Universally, it is accepted. The subconscious mind has an abundance power which can do miracles in your life.

Take care of your thought process so you can modify it in a proper way. If your thought process is in the right direction, your subconscious mind guides it in a better way. If your thought process is clear, constructive and harmonious, the magic of your subconscious mind reveals its powerful nature. As the subconscious mind works 24 X 7, whatever you want either success, prosperity, health or wealth, you can get much more efficiently by the proper use of it. The subconscious mind may support you in a better way.

Auto-suggestion, inner viewing, inner gauging and self-thinking influence the subconscious mind.

How it gets affected?

- Your regular thinking
- Your habit
- Your involvement
- Your attitude and behavior
- Your view of yourself
- Your view toward society
- Your conscious attention

The subconscious mind provides the solution to a problem, not in a quick or sudden way, but it takes time to analyze and respond in a significant way.

Courage counts

> *Success is not final, failure is not fatal: it is the courage to continue that counts.*
> **– Winston S. Churchill**

Every person should gain the courage to lead an empowered life.

It's a blend of bravery, integrity, perseverance, and intellectual acumen.

Throughout the day, we come across several examples. Whenever we hear the word courage, our mind gets filled up with many examples like
- A firefighter crossing across the fire
- A person crossing the physical barrier and climbing the harsh mountain top.

Whenever we mention courage, we highlight physical endurance/physical capability.

Other forms of courage are less discussed and known to the masses. There are different kinds of courage as well, like physical courage, intellectual courage, spiritual courage, social courage, etc. Physical courage means moving ahead despite the harm to one's own physical body. One exhibits physical capability beyond the standard limit. Physical courage comes from regular physical activities. It includes sports, physical exercise, yoga, etc. Doing these, their physical endurance increases.

> *Courage is resistance to fear, mastery of fear - not absence of fear.*
>
> **– Mark Twain**

Wilma Rudolph

She was fragile since birth. At the age of four, she became paralyzed due to a combination of diseases. Until 11 years, she could not walk without an orthopedic shoe. Even in this situation, she told

"I want to be the fastest woman on the track on this earth". At the age of 15, she met a coach, and said, "I want to be a woman on track " coach replied, "with this spirit, nobody can stop you". Her journey started, she won in different races one after other. Spirit and physical endurance increased day by day. In 1960, she became the fastest woman on this earth. This showed how a person goes beyond the boundary

> *Don't be afraid of your fears. They're not there to scare you. They're there to let you know that something is worth it.*
> – **C. JoyBell C.**

> *A ship is safe in harbor, but that's not what ships are for.*
> – **John A. Shedd**

Arunima Sinha

A national level volleyball player, Arunima Sinha, went through a tragedy and lost her left leg. She lost only the leg but not the larger vision and deep-hearted determination. She then decided to climb Mount Everest, by expanding her zone of self-respect with courage, dedication and determination. With regular practice, she conquered Mount Everest on 21st May 2013. She became the world's first Indian female amputee to climb Mount Everest. She turned the tragedy into a turning point in her life. In such a situation, a normal or common person may lose their heart and lead a low life. This is an example of bouncing back. It is the courage to counter adversity.

Courage to continue

KFC - After a number of failures, this brand becomes successful.

Edison - He tried a thousand times before he invented the electric bulb.

So, to excel in life, one should inculcate courage to move forward in tough conditions.

YOUR NOTES

8
NOW OR NEVER

> *Live as if you were to die tomorrow. Learn as if you were to live forever.*
>
> **– Mahatma Gandhi**

Time is never good or bad. It is up to you how you see your world and your work. Don't put much thought but act. Whether you like the work or not, just do it without considering the taste. You must have heard, each day is new and afresh; it contains a lot of opportunities in its womb, so don't lose to avail the opportunities before you. Undoubtedly, every moment is new and afresh, which has a lot of flings to endeavor. There will be nothing like this moment to accomplish in this universe. So, utilize the moment fully.

> *"My success just evolved from working hard at the business at hand each day."*
>
> **– Johnny Carson**

Ordinary men always claim the mood is not so good, as they will not do the work today. Next time I will do. Such people are mood-dependent or have no self-control or self-determination to do a particular work. Some people are environment or weather dependent. A slight change in the environment restricts them from working. They put all the blame on the environment. Wherever they go, they blame others. Such people have escaping tendencies. I have observed closely different educational organizations of higher studies, where most of the faculties had a doctorate degree and had exemplary academic records and accomplishments; even so, they were passive. They put the things for later. They were working and academically qualified but had a tendency to put the thing for next time. Most of them put the thing to do tomorrow and again for tomorrow. He/she won't do unless the pressure surmounts high.

Break your inner chain and be free. Live the moment, the **very present moment**, not tomorrow, not yesterday, not even today before noon or afternoon. If you follow the above principle, then only you will be a true activist or possible doer.

Be a pro in every work and do everything with a positive attitude.

Pro-reading

Pro-watching

> *Never lose faith in yourself that you can. You can do anything and everything. Practice hard; whether you live or die does not matter. You have to plunge in and work without thinking of the results.*
>
> **– Vivekanand**
>
> *"The minute you settle for less than you deserve, you get even less than you settled for."*
>
> **– Maureen Dowd**

What is pulling you back?

No doubt, we like to move ahead in life for prosperity and improvement. But many factors hold us from moving in the right direction. Success requires pace and perfection. Factors which hold us back are:

- Lack of ability to prioritize things.
- Lack of determination
- Lack of ambition
- Over anxiety
- Lack of opportunities and recognition
- Lack of self-respect
- Rusting of strength

There is always resistance when you do some new work. People like to take a decision but wait for the favorable condition to come.

> *"Well begun is half done."*
> **– Aristotle (Greek Philosopher)**

Spruce up the spirit

> *People often say that motivation doesn't last. Well, neither does bathing - that's why we recommend it daily.*
> **– Zig Ziglar**

Tune up the resources so you can walk through the ladder of progress. Do your own research about physical, mental, and spiritual progress. Try to make mind maps of all these and put them into black and white. Writing on paper clarifies our focuses, our objectives, our strategies, our planning and our process.

> *Give me six- hours to chop down a tree, and I will spend the first four hours sharping the axe.*
>
> **– Abraham Lincoln**

Revamp your wisdom

Rectify your deed

Cultivate the good

To elevate to the top.

Lift your emotion

So to reform your future.

Each person needs the same to improve their efficiency in their journey to the mission. In due course of time, they become dormant and then move slowly. They are exhausted. When people are worried or tense, many go to a bar and drink, which is a bad habit. It is better to sit down calmly and just watch the thoughts that come and go but don't resist the thought whichever comes and go. Let it come and go. Don't differentiate between good and evil. Just have attention to the inhalation and exhalation. If you resist it, then it will persist. Why do you worry so much? Every tide in a sea settles down. All things are changing in life. Have this belief deep into your heart.

Life is never perfect. You make plans and routines, and they need to be changed with the passage of time. But you must keep moving and flowing. Please keep taking decisions actively. Don't overthink before taking a decision. You are never too old to embark on a *new mission* in life. No doubt, you may invent a newer version of yourself.

Working Ability/Efficiency

Spirit can be improved

Spirit can be enhanced

Spirit improves in a spiral way or, you can say, in a pyramidal way. Its base is constituted of physical, mental, and emotional well-being. As the base provides more energy and support, the height of the spirit will be more.

The three bases of spirit include physical, mental, and emotional activities; as you improve these three, the height of spirit will proportionately increase.

Regularity is reasonable, but if you do similar work simultaneously at regular intervals, it leads you to be monotonous or similar to a machine. If you fix a particular routine, your working ability and creativity go down. Your physical strength goes down. You become exhausted. You are exhausted not only physically but mentally and spiritually as well. In one of my counseling program, one asked, "Is it possible to revamp our spirit?"

I was very enthusiastic about doing the thing that was before me. I had a lot of dreams and a lot of courage to do many things. Now with time, I feel exhausted. Those dreams of teenage have now faded away. The dreams seem to be far away. The dreams become dormant now. The big question is that the spirit has gone down. The energy is dormant, it settled down and am feeling low.

This is the case for a large population. Many of us forget the childhood dreams that we had aspired to be. With the passage of time, we crossed a number of hurdles and opportunities.

You do need to understand the causes or reasons.

Put the dreams on paper and again plan in a better way and work on that but don't lose the dream.

Be Unpredictable

If anyone predicts anything about yourself that means you are working as a machine, not as a human.

Get Set Go

Don't wait for an ideal situation to come to start or work on a new idea. Don't over-prepare. If you are in bed, stand up; move if you are standing.

Likewise, embrace the spirit of action, it's essential to seize the moment and dive into new ventures with zest. The perfect time to act on an idea or a concept is now, not in some distant, flawless future which may never arrive. Over-preparation can be a form of procrastination, a barrier to the action and innovation. Whether it's a spark of creativity at midnight or a sudden insight while on a walk, the key is to move with purpose and passion. Every step taken is a step closer to realization, and every moment of hesitation is an opportunity missed. So, rise from contemplation, stride forward from stillness, and let the momentum of your actions carry you towards your success.

M – Motivate

O – Own

V – Valuable

E – Energy

And go-go AHEAD

Keep going

Keep doing

Keep working

And keep it up

Whenever you feel the momentum or urge or idea to do something, do it at that moment itself; otherwise, it fades away.

Never wait,

Never wait,

Waiting always means wasting your time.

Absolutely! Seizing the moment is essential. When inspiration strikes or motivation surges, acting promptly can lead to meaningful progress. Waiting often dissipates that initial energy.

Remember, now is the perfect time to take action! Whether it's pursuing a goal, expressing gratitude, or making a positive change, embrace the present and move ahead as You are a NOBLE ONE.

YOUR NOTES

www.ingramcontent.com/pod-product-compliance
Lightning Source LLC
LaVergne TN
LVHW041543070526
838199LV00046B/1819